Suffering Silently

Thanks for your support
S. Williams

SUDIE WILLIAMS

ISBN 978-1-64515-975-9 (paperback)
ISBN 978-1-64515-976-6 (digital)

Christian Faith Publishing, Inc.
832 Park Avenue
Meadville, PA 16335
www.christianfaithpublishing.com

Printed in the United States of America

Contents

Acknowledgments

Special thanks to my husband Glenn, daughter Peachy, and son-in-law Thomas. To my siblings, mentors, World Overcomers Church and also to Christian Faith Publishing Company I appreciate your support.

In Memory of
Every Grieving Family

We would like to express our heartfelt sympathy to all of the families who are **suffering silently,** due to several random acts of violence, sickness, accidents, or natural causes etc. all around the world.

Those tragedies have affected your lives forever. The enjoyment, of having your loved ones here for a while, then watching them go away, will forever remain in your heart and on your mind.

We believe **all** lives matters. **All** lives are valuable. Memories are priceless and unforgettable. You should treasure those precious moments, for comfort, strength and serenity.

If feasible, do something in honor of your deceased family members or friends. This will keep their legacy alive so their names will always be remembered locally or nationally.

Let the world know, they are gone but never forgotten.

Our thoughts and prayers are with you daily. Although it going to take some time for healing to occur, we still wish you peace.

Once again, please accept our deepest condolences.

The Williams Family

Overview

Have you ever been in so much pain that you couldn't tell anyone what was going on? Living with hurt, pain, struggles and headaches for the past several months, while keeping it concealed from your relatives and friends, has been overwhelming.

Longing to share those problems with a person who is trustworthy, dependable, nonbiased, and supportive seemed very difficult to do. Also looking for someone who would be able to keep your personal information confidential was even more challenging to find. Prayerfully this individual would be able to love, respect and embrace you, during this desperate time period, until the situation was resolved.

Finding no one available to listen, inspire, or provide comfort and encouragement, when you needed it the most, created more depression. *Suffering silently,* feeling hopeless and friendless, made you feel unloved and unappreciated.

Were you sitting around waiting for that one phone call, text, email, or letter saying "Forgive me, I am so sorry" from the people who had caused your pains? When you did not hear from them, did you sink deeper into depression? No doubt there were many times you tried to ignore the issue by praying or doing other activities. Were you able to get eight hours of rest without some type of sleep aid? Have you cried yourself to sleep or said this is the last time I'm going to "worry" over this thing? Trying to relax, did you listen to your favorite music, drank hot or cold liquids or took hot showers, hoping to forget about your enemies or accusers? When was your pains the worse? Have you planned to move on mentally and physically but could not make the effort to do so?

Death

Have you ever experienced the death of a loved ones and grieved months or years later? You were so attached that now, in his or her absence, it is still hard to readjust to the silence; so you cannot freely move on. The memories of the past still linger vividly in your mind and heart. Your cries have been uncontrollable at times. You had taken different types of medications to help you get over the tragic unexpected or expected death. Yet nothing seemed to ease the heart-aches or answer the unexplained questions: "Why did this occur? Why did this happen to my child, pet, parent(s), or religious person, etc.?"

Those questions went on seemingly unresolved. Did you seek comfort in people or things hoping to convince yourself that some-day the pains would lessen? Were there a longing and yearning for any positive words of comfort to your bleeding heart? Please take note that you are not the only one who felt that way.

There are some people who has never fully gotten over the death of a loved one, especially if it was a spouse, child, or parent. It is still very hard to even look at some of their personal belongings. You have to find a way to talk it out, socialize, or even engage in an activity that could help bring comfort, if not closure. Whatever choice you might have chosen, the fact remains, you are still *suffering silently.*

Loss of a Pet

Losing a pet can be very difficult to handle. It is a special kind of grieving because your animal became part of the family. Perhaps you spent a lot of time and/or money on the upkeep of this cuddly creature before it passed away.

People said you would eventually get over it. After all, it was just an animal. A spouse or parent stated he/she would buy another one to replace the one you lost. You were thankful for their generous idea, but you realized that another pet would only take the space but not the place of the one that you lost.

The joy of seeing your pet playing around and the attachment you had left a void in your heart. It has been hard to readjust without their sound or movement being heard.

The memories were so priceless because your pet was a comfort keeper, protector, and often it was your best friend. You *suffered silently* because you missed your animal. Realizing you must eventually press forward to receive mental healing, it just seems hard to do right now.

Miscarriage/Still Birth

Did you and your spouse/mate try so hard to become parents? Finally, you rejoiced at the news that you were pregnant. It was a joy telling everyone you were going to become parents. Counting down 9 months until the expected delivery date, for the newest addition, brought such excitement to the family.

Then your pregnancy turned in the opposite direction. You went to the family doctor, expecting, praying, and hoping for a good report. But instead you were devastated upon hearing the news that you had a miscarriage.

The thought of losing a child, the pains of not being able to produce a child or to be called Mom and Dad ripped through your very soul. All of those pressures, along with the question when people asked, "Did you have your baby yet?" followed by hearing the words, "Oh I'm so sorry" pierced your heart. Your eyes became filled with tears as your heart gripped with internal sorrows because, only a mother knows the depth of the hurt. Those pains took months or years to go away because you were constantly seeing other people's children and wishing you could only embrace your own child. Hearing others say "perhaps you should try again later" added more mental stress.

Who really understands the agony of an empty womb and a throbbing heart after such an experience? You felt that was your only hope and possibility of becoming parents. So now you walk around mundane, feeling empty inside, while *suffering silently*.

Abortion/Unwanted Pregnancy

So you got pregnant deliberately hoping to trap your spouse or partner into a long, lasting relationship. Did you think a child would make your marriage stronger and more productive? Are you the woman who got impregnated by mistake, carelessness, rape or incest? If the conception occurred, not by choice, most certainly there were mixed emotions and decisions that had to be dealt with.

However the pregnancy occurred, most options appeared negatively after discovering your significant other did not want a child, causing more worries and confusion.

After much agonizing thoughts day after day and night after night, you decided to secretly move forward with the abortion. Fear and guilt griped your heart. Somehow you convinced yourself this was the right choice to make at this particular time in your life, due to hardship and timing. Feeling selfish and irresponsible, you struggled with the idea of abortion (weighing the options repeatedly) until scheduling an appointment to have the procedure done.

Since that time whether several weeks, months or even years later, memories of the abortion is still painful. You often feel sad while crying inwardly. The agony of wondering what your child could have grown up to become has left you brokenhearted as you *suffer silently* blaming yourself for the loss of life.

Teenage/Adolescence Pregnancy

So you hung out with your significant other on a planned date. Everything went well at first. The evening was being excitingly filled with dinner, movie, dancing etc. and the time seemed perfect for you both. Your partner was making sure this occasion would be very special and memorable.

Later that day or night, you two decided to embrace each other's company alone just a little while longer. You began with a hug, a kiss, then fondling, which later led to sex. The music sounded so romantic and made the mood just right for intimacy. The two of you enjoyed the activities with fun, excitement, and expectations of this reoccurring again soon.

After all the sex and romance ceased, if you were a virgin, you then realized your virginity was no longer pure. You had done what so many other teens have done. If you had sex being pressured against your wishes, yet giving in to your partner, just to show your love and loyalty, probably left you with great concerns.

At any rate, after the lovemaking was over, you discovered in a few weeks that your cycle did not appear. Being afraid, you desperately prayed that it would show up late this time. However, it didn't and now you realize that pregnancy had occurred. You were scared to tell your partner for fear he did not want children at this age, did not want children with you, or did not want children at all.

You both *suffered silently*, wondering "how a child will have an impact" on your future dreams, educational goals or create a financial hardship. You might be considering if you should have an abortion, give the child up for adoption, get married, or simply raise the child with the support of others.

For the welfare of the child, speak with your family members immediately upon the discovery of your pregnancy. Make sound decisions carefully and wisely. Seek counseling, guidance and support from reliable caregivers.

Peer Pressure Disagreement

Teenagers or young adults could *suffer silently* due to peer pressure of high demands. Other or older peers sometimes pressure youth into doing things that's immoral or contrary to their family's beliefs.

They are *suffering silently* while deciding whether or not to join in just to fit into the group. Should they simply walk away and be considered unsociable and unacceptable amongst the crowd? They might become isolated, and if teased on social media, he/she might sometimes do physical or psychological harm to themselves.

Being pressured frequently can lead to suicide. Youth become prey to bullies as well. They are afraid to tell anyone because of threats from their bullies. Sometimes youth join gangs to be accepted or to earn fast money. They keep it a secret from their parents, school officials, or best friends. Once initiated, then later he/she decide to get out of the gang, they fear for their lives and their relatives safety. So internally they *suffered silently*, unsure of what to do or who to talk to.

Don't be afraid to talk to your school counselors or trusted family members. Seek ways to protect yourself from danger.

Parent/Child Disagreement

Parents sometimes put extra pressure on their child/children to perform in their dreams and visions rather than allowing them to pursue their own goals and desires. Some parents may even threaten their children to get involved in the family's business, even though that was not their child's current aspiration or passion. After becoming adults, parents should not dictate how people must live their lives.

Typically, children do not like to displease or disrespect their parents. 'Most young adults envision being out on their own, working on the type of job that interest them or attend the college of their choice. They do not want to walk in their parents footsteps and may have shared this concern with other trusted people. However, he/she may reluctantly comply with their parents' wishes for a certain amount of time while *suffering silently*.

Young adults should have the rights to venture out on their own, to explore, and to discover their strengths, qualities, and abilities. However, they might be able to use some of their parents' ideas while working with other agencies outside the family's business. Refusing to tell anyone because they didn't want to upset or anger their parents, he/she kept the unpleasant feeling internally while *suffering silently*.

Relinquished Parental Rights

Perhaps you were *suffering silently,* feeling guilty and ashamed, for giving up your rights as parents to your child/children, due to some particular reason. Did you relinquish custody due to neglect, poverty, poor parenting skills, bad judgment or substance abuse etc?

Although the child/children might be well cared for by relatives, foster care agency, or adoption, the innate yearning of a mother's love still cries out for their child from time to time. Especially when the mother is sober or alone she often *suffers silently.*

Mentally you have tried to move on however, there is always the reminder of abandonment. Remembering the children brings about a desire to see, touch, hold, or even play with them. Feeling regretful and neglectful, wondering if the children will grow up to dislike being fostered by others, has you *suffering silently.*

After repeatedly telling yourself you were not a good Mom or Dad, there was an increase usage of prescription and OTC medications to help cope with the memories and embarrassment. Unintentionally, this might have later led to your substance abuse. Deep down you are hurting and *suffering silently* hoping the pains would someday go away.

Talking to a psychiatrist, therapist or social worker may help ease your tension and /or frustration.

Decision Making for Senior or Disabled Relatives

The elderly, veterans, and disabled are a major concern in our society. They are very vulnerable and often forgotten. We realize these groups need trained people who can care for them according to their overall needs.

The question whether or not to admit your family member into a long-term care facility can be agonizing, even though there are workers there 24/7 to care for those specific individuals.

After researching, you discussed the cost and thought about ways to save money by keeping your loved ones at home in their familiar environment. You anticipated other people would come over to help care for your senior or disabled person. Since there was no one available to help, due to various reasons, there were choices that had to be made.

Sometimes the elderly can become too demanding, or they need a higher level of care than you could provide for them. Looking for the right housing with a vacancy could take months to find.

After visiting several facilities, a placement was chosen for him/ her to live outside of their comfort zone. Although feeling guilty about the living arrangements amongst strangers, you knew this was the right thing to do under the circumstances. This was a very difficult decision to make which caused you to *suffer silently* while the transition was being made.

If it was your disabled child who had to be admitted to a housing facility, the pain could be even worse. Although communicating with him/her on regular bases, you still *suffer silently* because of pressure, guilt and the inability to provide the services he/she need for daily survival. It is such a big challenge to take care of children/young adults with special mental or physical disabilities.

Try talking to counselors, therapist, senior care groups or individuals who had to admit their relatives into a residential facility. Hopefully you can find support to help your family adjust to their new living environment.

Elderly Abuse

Most seniors are placed in long-term care facilities against their wishes. Because the elderly require so much medical care which cannot be provided at their homes, the relatives are left with the decision to place them into a senior-care facility.

You should be very selective when choosing the right placement for your loved ones. Make appointments to visit the elderly care homes on several occasions at various times of the day. There are good quality assisted living centers in the area, and there are some with lesser standards. When you visit, not only should you observe the other residents, but watch the staff's interactions with the seniors as well.

Senior-care homes are sometimes reported to local law enforcement or social service agencies for abuse and/or neglect. These residents *suffer silently* because either they cannot talk or maybe they are afraid. They also may suffer verbal, physical, or emotional abuse by the staff or other seniors. Make sure you check on your relative daily or often as possible to ensure they are safe.

Always be observant of senior citizens. If you suspect elderly abuse in his/her home, report it to the local officials.

At no time should our elderly be mistreated or disrespected because of age, race, or health issues.

Engagement/Lies/Deceit

Being deeply in love with anticipation of friendship, courtship, engagement, then eventually getting married is very exciting. Ever envision being united and living happily ever after, while raising a small family for that "perfect" soul mate or soul ties, for life? There is so much excitement dreaming about exchanging vows someday with that special someone.

After accepting the proposal, did your partner begin to exhibit many unbelievable flaws? Were investments (money, time etc.) made and now it has all been wasteful or a learning experience? How far into the relationship was discovery made that your ex fiancé was a constant liar, deceiver, jealous stalker, molester, compulsive spender, criminal, or lazy? Was he/she heavily indebted, suffered from mental disorders, had other children, or been previously married, etc.? When did you learn there were little commonality? Also were there other things learned about him/her via social media, cell phone messages, personal items or friends?

As new information developed, what emotions did you display? Obviously some of the feelings were devastation, speechless or just plain outraged that your engagement had to be cancelled. Close observation quickly determined that person would not be the right one. Blaming yourself for not listening and responding to constructive criticism early into the relationship caused you to *suffer silently* after the breakup.

Dating deals with emotions. Be very cautious in choosing a mate for life. Find out as much information about your significant other's past and goals for the future, before making a commitment that will impact your future.

Infidelity

Your wedding day finally arrived. You both were sincere about the longevity of marriage by stating the words "until death do us apart." After the ceremony and honeymoon was over, a new journey began as Mr. and Mrs. Always and Forever.

It was months or year later before your spouse behavior began to change. He/she appeared distant, uninterested in family time, always on the go, constantly making excuses, inconsistencies etc. As those behaviors continued repeatedly, it prompted some personal investigation. The search began by looking for several items that would prove something indecent was going on.

Although you couldn't find anything concrete at first, your suspicion believed infidelity was taking place because the romantic sexual encounters decreased. Then came the late arrivals, lying, lack of focus, always excusing himself/herself to go and use the restroom, whispering while on the phone, or always saying "I can't talk now".

Eventually there were so many red flags you knew without a doubt that he/she was cheating. As many thoughts came to mind, your heart sunk into disbelief. Hesitantly and privately you had to confine in someone. After disclosing the unfaithfulness to a trusted individual, you began to *suffer silently* as to what steps should be taken that would least affect the family. There were financial arrangements, custody issues and other pertinent matters that had to be considered.

Being seen in public, you were always viewed as the perfect happy couple. You expected this marriage to last a lifetime, however, you *suffered silently* when your perfect soul mate became your separated mate.

Seek marriage support groups or seek family therapy counseling who can help with transition, guidance and decision making.

Separation/Divorce

Have you gone through or is currently going through marital breakup and/or divorce? The heartbreak from separation of the families could be tragic for both parents and children. This brings division in relationships, marriages, couple's friendship, discipline skills, parenting styles, community, and so much more.

Often women are more vulnerable to get hurt through separation. There is so much at stake. Her feelings of anger, sometimes guilt, frustration, worries, anxieties, embarrassment, loneliness, financial hardship, fear of the unknown, lack of stability, single parenting, homelessness, etc. could cause her heartaches and grief. Often getting up early and going to bed late she struggle to hide herself and true feelings from the family or public. Anxiety attacks or nervous breakdowns happen due to excessive stress, decreased appetite, or overeating. At first she tries to cope by isolation, shopping or engaging in social interaction with others hoping to experience love, hugs, laughter, comfort and connection.

During separation, it is often easier for some men to move on with their lives. They realize the marriage is over and has no interest in restoring the union or desire to help keep the family intact. He may quickly move on to another relationship, putting the past behind him. On some occasions, the husband may be the one hurting the most. He may suggest they both seek counseling, hoping therapy will help keep the family together. Long months of separation (if the relationship is not soon restored) could lead to alcohol, drugs, sexual misconduct, etc. Isolation is usually short-lived with men who experience separation or divorce. They can mentally bounce back by attending a gym, club, hang out late with buddies, flirt with others, watch porn, etc. However, the woman in the relationship is yet hoping, praying, looking, and wishing that things are soon restored so the family can heal. While *suffering silently,* she cry, pray, worry and sacrifice her time, talent, and abilities to make sure everyone's needs at home are met.

For your own peace of mind, health and safety, if you need to depart, do so peacefully as possible. There are divorce counseling groups in many areas, including some churches. They encourage people to share their issues of concern. Seek out people you can talk to who will lead you forward to a road of hope, healing and happiness. Many people have proven that there is life after divorce. You can be one of them.

Rape/Incest

Have you ever been sexually abused (implying **any kind** of sexual behaviors without your consent) from a stranger, acquaintance or family member? Were you fondled but not penetrated or ever forced to touch or look at a person private parts? Did someone bind your feet or mouth (so you could not scream for help or run away?) Has nude photos been taken of you against your knowledge or were there, at any time, coercion into performing sexual activities while being a minor? How often was money or gifts offered in exchange for inappropriate physical contacts from the rapist/molester?

As a result of those unsolicited encounters, are you *suffering silently* because it is a personal violation? Were there doubts no one would believe it occurred or perhaps investigators would not be able to find enough information to prove it was indeed rape?

How frighten did you become thinking pregnancy might occur from the attack? Does reoccurring nightmares prevent you from sleeping in the dark or using the restroom at night? Are you mentally and physically *suffering silently*, wondering how to disclose these brutal attacks and the offender who did the molestation/rape?

All those incidents are illegal. They should be reported to your local authorities. At no time should your body be violated. This includes sex that was consensual, but your partner became so rough it caused excessive pains which required medical attention. You need to speak out immediately, recalling all of the details to law enforcement and medical personnel, while the horrible crime is fresh on your mind.

Infertility

Women who are barren or cannot give birth to children for various reasons often *suffer silently* in a painful way. When they are around other children, see a pregnant woman or hear the announcement that a female is expecting, she once again begin to *suffer silently*, desperately wanting to have a baby.

This can be very difficult after trying repeatedly to have a child but somehow she is unable to do so. Some women start to blame themselves or their spouse/partner. If the man really wants children, he may put pressure on the female to perform more often, hoping each month that his dream of becoming a father comes true.

Men can *suffer silently* too feeling inadequate that he is incapable of producing or fathering a child especially a son. If he discovers it is his "fault" his woman cannot conceive, he may resort to medical advice or become silent, preferring not to attend events where children are present. Father's Day and Mother's Day can be especially hard when they long to hear the words Mom and Dad coming from their biological child/children.

There are many agencies that can help with fostering and/or adopting children. If you have the space in your home and love in your heart to give guidance, nurture, love, support, and care, please contact the Department of Human Services or adoption agencies.

You don't have to *suffer in silence*. There are many children in foster care, waiting for loving parents and a loving home. Research and discover what is best for you both.

Erectile Dysfunction

This is another area where men really *suffer silently* because he may feel insecure when performing sexually with his wife/partner. Because men are such macho, embarrassment may occur if they cannot reach the peak of their sexual performance.

Men *suffer silently* with this condition for various reasons. Certain medications, mental and/or medical conditions tend to make this problem worse, affect their ego and self-esteem.

Make an appointment to talk with your doctor, do research, live a healthy lifestyle and reduce alcohol intake. Inform your doctor of any physical or psychological conditions you may have. Learn to avoid things that would increase your stress level.

There are medications, and perhaps treatments, the physician may prescribe depending on your health and age. Remember to do self-care by exercising, eating healthy, and quitting smoking.

The specialist team may consist of your primary care doctor, clinical psychologist, psychiatrist, cardiologist and urologist etc. Prayerfully, working as a team, they can help find a workable solution to prevent you from *suffering silently*.

Sexual Orientation

In past years many people including Hollywood stars, professional athletics, politicians, news reporters, priests, etc., have revealed they are a part of the LGBT community. Some chose this lifestyle in spite of their family's moral or religious belief. We live in a society where everyone has a right to choose even if it is contrary to what you were originally taught.

There are some people who would like to come forth and disclose their sexual preference. They *suffer silently* because of the stigmatism and disbelief others would think about them. These individual fear they would be stereotyped, harassed, unaccepted, or uninvited. He/she want others to know they feel trapped in their body with the gender they were born with, and mentally they want to be free to disclose themselves.

Some desire to be physically changed and equally accepted into society. Therefore, being ashamed to come forth, they hide their feelings as they *suffer silently*.

Perhaps you could confine in a trusted friend, counselor, or research support groups who can encourage you to express your feelings.

Addiction
(Alcohol and Drug) Abuse

Lately you have shown many instances of excessive talking, over sleeping, fidgeting, disorienting and inattention which have resulted in several careless mistakes being made.

Your inner circle had begun asking questions that you were refusing to answer or admitting the secret addiction to substance abuse. Being precautious, you tried to hide your breath odor with various mouth fresheners, avoided your supervisor, or wore long sleeves to cover needle marks.

Often fearing an overdose may occur, someday you might get caught drunk from alcohol or high on narcotics, have you nervous and *suffering silently*. Due to denial and unwillingness to share your abusive problem with others, counseling seems to be your least concern. Yet there are worries that those dependent chemicals could led to the possibility of losing your job, marriage, relationship or respect in the community.

Family and friends would like to offer assistance, upon disclosing you have a problem and really want to seek their help. Also there are drug, alcohol, and substance abuse agencies that provide training to help people cope with life hardship or to eliminate their bad habits when they are ready for a sincere lifestyle change.

Depression/
Anxiety Medications

Do you wake up feeling drained and exhausted in all areas of your life? Have life been better or worse after spending lots of money on doctor visits and medications? Are you constantly worried, confused, unhappy, depressed, distressed, or at wits end?

Anyone who *suffers silently* may not know who to turn to when there is an emotional crisis. They prefer not to talk with a psychiatrist or psychologist for fear he/she may be characterized as mentally ill. Also it makes a person feels uncomfortable sharing private information with a stranger. Being reluctant, you don't want any personal problems to go on your personnel or school records. Weighing all the options, people often put off scheduling an appointment with those professionals as long a possible.

Desperately longing for a restful night sleep, are you taking all kinds of over the counter sleep aid medications? However, the depression and anxiety still causes insomnia, migraines, decreased appetite for nutritious meals, or overeating unhealthy food items.

Due to high levels of stress, are you *suffering silently* over things, situations, people, and issues that are apparently uncontrollably? While praying and hoping for things to get better soon, you adjust to the misery by doing other things legal or illegal, moral or immoral. Keeping a low profile often help your symptoms remain unnoticeable to others.

Talk to your healthcare provider and inform them about what is or what is not working. If you are currently under a physician care, it is recommended that your prescription medications be taken, as prescribed, without skipping or discontinuing dosages, without their approval.

Medical Condition
(Sickness/Disease)

After taking the tests or exams, then impatiently waiting for the results to come back negative, it seemed to take forever.

The day arrived when the doctor called to confirm your identity. While waiting nervously to hear the report, fear gripped your heart. The results confirmed the medical team's suspicion of a terminal illness or growth (tumor). Wondering if the disease was treatable or life threatening you might have cried, panicked, screamed or even fainted upon hearing the diagnosis.

The shock and disbelief that something of this sort would ever happen to you were simply unbelievable. Pacing the floor, being indecisive about who to tell and who the bad news should be kept confidential from, cause you to *suffer silently*.

Eventually family members and close friends were told. They tried to offer comfort and hope but you were the one who was *suffering silently* and had to undergo necessary tests, procedures, surgery and treatments. If the condition was life threatening you may have asked people to pray for a positive outcome and a speedily recovery.

Because of your spouse/partner's unfaithfulness, did you contract STD? Ever wonder how many others had been infected by him/her? Were there insurance or funds available to purchase the medication needed for your treatment? Being mentally battered, with so much bitterness and resentment, gave you the desire to separate yourself. Concerns remain as whether trust, honesty, and faithfulness can ever be restored. While curious about so many issues and thoughts of "what if", has caused you to *suffer silently*. Realizing there are proactive choices and decisions about your health and well-being, that need to be made, has created devastation in your life and lack of trust for the individual. Seek spiritual and medical advice. Do the necessary treatments that lead to healing and recovery.

Suicidal Thoughts

Are you so tired, weary, worn, despondent, abandoned, rejected, neglected, abused, unloved, unattractive, unsociable, discouraged, confused, worried, troubled, ashamed, unappreciated and/or feeling unwanted?

All of these emotions are unhealthy thoughts and feelings that have a negative impact on your life. Individuals tend to see the glass half empty instead of half full. He/she also can't imagine the possibility of a bright sunshiny day with peace, joy, love and living happily ever after.

Somehow you must pray and put your mind over these matters. Each person must let go of negativity and replace it with positivity in order to get his/her emotions under control.

People *suffer silently* when they refuse to seek professional help or counseling from trusted loved ones. We can agree it is very difficult to get over an unexpected death, divorce, job loss, terminal illness, etc. You must somehow remember good and bad things happen to all of us. Time and therapy can help bring about healing in most cases.

Holding things within yourselves and *suffer silently* alone is far worse than disclosing your feelings. Invite others into your world to help you cope with problems that seem unbearable.

There are Suicide hotlines in your area. Please seek help immediately. To unwind, simply pause from your daily activities and go outside to behold the beauty of nature.

Finance/Loss of Income

Are you are working exhausting hours, yet lagging behind in bills and constantly struggling from one paycheck to the next one, trying to make provisions for your family? Is the collection agency calling at all times of day? Are your checks being garnished for back pay? Has the lack of money become your number one concern right now?

Having to borrow money from other people is quite embarrassing. You are *suffering silently* because your heavy debts keep you in lack or barely having enough money remaining each payday. Regardless of your efforts to get ahead, there is always a need for more cash.

It appears there is no financial relief in sight until the children are grown, loans are paid off or inheritance money becomes available. So in the meantime, you long for the day when it will be convenient and comfortably living on your fixed income.

To help offset your financial obligations, make a budget or seek debt consolidation solutions. Reduce unnecessary spending or seek part time employment, if feasible with your schedule and health, to earn extra income. Pay off credit card expenses one at a time beginning with the small debt elimination. Spend less money shopping at fast food or department stores. If possible, buy used items instead of new ones. It is best to rent, rather than purchase, items like video games, movies etc.

If you have a gambling problem, consider seeking a gambling addiction agency that may help eliminate unnecessary spending. Also, research to see if there are financial planners in your area that can help you get out of debt by budgeting your money.

Disabled/Special Needs

If you have a disability or perhaps a family member that has a special need, most likely you *suffer silently* every day. Watching people stare at you can cause emotional stress. It's unfortunate that you have to deal with the disability but to notice people pointing or whispering about you can bring out negative emotions that should be avoided.

You imagined life without the disability or what things could be done if you didn't have it. Having limitations in different areas such as cognitively, emotionally, visually, and/or hearing can be hurtful. Some individuals use medical devices or equipment that is noticeable. Perhaps you felt ashamed or got tired of people asking questions about your condition. Constantly repeating the same information may have caused frustration which led to your *suffering silently*.

It is important to remember we all are different, unique, and special in our ways. Even identical twins can have different characteristics and behaviors. We must appreciate everyone even those with limited abilities. However, you should not let your limitations hinder you from reaching your goals, dreams, and fullest potential. Only negative thinking can hinder you. Talk to others who have challenges and learn how they are coping with life's difficult issues.

Foster Care

There are too many kids living in foster care for various reasons because some counties have few licensed homes. When placements are found, the children are usually uprooted from their familiar environment and often placed in the care of strangers or put into other relatives' crowded homes.

When the child is still school aged, he/she may have to transfer to a new school district which can be fearful and stressful. Having to find new teachers and make new friends can cause the youth to *suffer silently* wanting to be with peers in their current neighborhood.

Being away from their biological parents and labeled as "foster child" also triggers behavior issues. While some individuals are mistreated in foster homes, they are afraid to tell anyone for fear of punishment or lack of nourishment. Therefore, many of them *suffer silently*, wanting and wishing their parents would receive the proper training and resources needed to reunite them with their family members.

There is a saying "It takes a village to raise a child." I agree with that statement. Each person wants to be loved, accepted, nurtured and respected. Adults should speak life, blessings, affirmation, and positive words of encouragement into the lives of these vulnerable, helpless, and innocent ones.

If you are interested in fostering or adoption, please contact your local Department of Social Services or independent foster care agencies to see if you qualify.

Military Spouses/
Military Veterans

America is a great place to live because we have so many privileges that other countries do not have. There is freedom of choice and citizen rights on many topics. Being united with different opinions and ideas on certain key issues, still enables us to be unique and powerful as a nation.

Everyone should stop to salute all of our brave men and women of the military. They fight daily for our freedom and safety. There are thousands of brave fallen heroes. We commend the surviving families, as they *suffer silently* daily, but especially on Memorial Day and Veteran's Day, for their relatives' loyalty, sacrifice, service and devotion to their country.

Soldiers are often deployed. The spouses are left behind to care for both the household expenses and the children. Their absence on holidays, birthdays, and anniversaries can be very difficult. They *suffer silently*, wishing their husbands/wives were here to share in the festival occasions. Deployment can be lengthy and draining for both spouses causing them to *suffer silently* mentally and physically. Sometimes the deployed soldier receives counseling to deal with the separation. They often count the days to their family's joyful reunification.

There are various activities and workshops the military offer to help the remaining spouse adjust to military life with support.

Military veterans *suffer silently* on regular basis. Many are wounded—physically, mentally, psychologically, and financially. Some of them *suffer silently* due to their permanent loss of limbs while others may have severe psychotic behaviors and nightmares resulting in separation, divorce or suicide.

Due to budget cuts, insurance, and other issues, some veterans do not receive the proper care and medications that they need. Often there is a long wait list before they can be seen by the physician and be properly diagnosed. Some are homeless while others have little food.

After honorably serving their country, they should be eligible for the best quality of care in a reasonable amount of time. It is inexcusable for our veterans to die or become homeless due to lack of care, finance or inability to receive an early detection appointment from a veteran medical center.

Bullying

Bullying can be detrimental to people's lives. He/she is often terrified and scared to go out to certain events for fear of being threatened or beaten by the bullies. They usually attack alone or in groups.

Years ago, violence in schools were increasing, especially among special need youths. Teenagers can be attacked via social media and live in fear for their lives. Because the individual refuse to tell anyone, he/she *suffer silently*. Some resort to suicide just to end the torture of being threaten on regular basis.

No one should have to live in this type of fear. If you are being harassed by anyone, including family members, report it to someone trustworthy who will help you escape from harm and violence.

Get help immediately; don't delay. Do not attempt to handle the bully alone because you might get hurt. Be watchful at all times and try not to go out alone. It is better to speak up rather than get beat up.

Domestic Violence

Are you in a relationship wherein you are being physically, verbally, emotionally, sexually or psychologically abused? Have you been physically abused which may consists of being beaten, slapped, kicked or, punched by your supposed to be lover? Has there been verbal abuse such as being cursed out, called names, yelled at, degraded, or threaten? Do you dread the physical contacts because your partner forces you to have sex or make you have sex in undesirable ways?

Perhaps you are afraid to tell someone for fear he/she may leave you, beat you again, put you out of the home, or stop giving you money. Living in an abusive environment, constantly being hurt and painfully *suffering silently* causes extreme misery. Your desire for freedom is to get out of the relationship safely then end this turmoil. However, it has been difficult finding confidence toward making the first step to get up and simply walk away.

All these types of abuse mentioned above should never be tolerated. If you are in a hostile relationship, you need to get help fast. Try to confide with a trusted person who can help lead you to the right agency that protects against domestic violence. Be aware of threats also. Tell local authorities about all of them and how dangerous your partner can become at various times. Ask about restraining orders and custody issues. Protect yourself and your family at all times. Ensure your car and house doors are locked and secured. It is wise to inquire about security alarm systems. Monitor your phone calls and doorbell rings.

Utilize every precaution to avoid the abuser. Be cautious about getting lured back into the relationship unless your abusive partner receives anger management counseling, and/or medications to get the behaviors under control. Your family safety and well-being must take top priority.

Wrongfully Accused

Can you imagine being wrongfully accused for something you did not do? Will it cost you to lose your job or marriage, breakup of a relationship or end a business deal? Your character and reputation could be affected if jail time is involved. How much humiliation will this cause an innocent person?

People are being wrongfully accused for various reasons every day. This causes damage—psychologically, emotionally, physically, spiritually, mentally, and financially. Were the allegations so hurtful the suffering felt endless?

Men try to be macho, and thus, they cry inwardly rather than outwardly. Women may have nervous breakdowns because she is ashamed and always have to dig deeper to prove their innocence. Therefore, they *suffer silently* when blamed even though all the evidences show they are innocent.

When you have not done anything wrong, hold your head up, fight for justice, continue to tell the truth, seek legal and psychological counseling.

Incarcerated

What other group of people *suffer silently* every day for years other than those who are incarcerated? Whether they are put behind bars willfully, deliberately, foolishly, neglectfully, regretfully, misconduct, insanity issues, or self defense, each person still *suffers silently* individually.

After being locked away to himself/herself and had time to think about the crime committed, he/she began to realize there were better choices that could have been made. Although it is too late now, several regretted what they did. Others were embarrassed because they got caught, and still there were some who felt personal revenge would solve the problem regardless of what legal charges they may face.

Being alone gives the individuals time to really soul search what their future will look like. Many will *suffer silently* while carrying the label of being a prisoner, felon, sex offender, rapist, child molester, thief, burglar, drug dealer, embezzler, etc. for the rest of their life.

There is so much to consider now that their freedom has been captured. He/she can no longer attend family gatherings, participate in holiday events, go dining, or shopping at their favorite places. Each prisoner *suffers silently*, longing to be home with family during special occasions.

There is a lot that goes into the legal process of prisoners being released. It can take years before the incarcerated is considered for parole or even released. Most inmates hope and pray their case will be reviewed and granted discharge. They *suffer silently* waiting for the message stating freedom has been approved because their incarcerated time has been completed.

While family members do not support the criminal's willful misconduct (unless self-defense), they still keep in contact with their relative. Adjusting to confinement, while *suffering silently*, inmates anxiously wait for letters, cards, photos, and/or money from their family and friends.

Holidays/Mealtimes/ Special Occasions Stress

It has been stated that depression always spike during the holiday seasons. People hold lots of memories that is dear to their hearts. The past infiltrate our minds and hearts as we long for the presence of our absent loved ones. Stress, worry, sickness, and depression all seem to kick in at once during these tender moments.

All holidays are important to remember, but those that stand out the most are birthdays, New Year, Christmas, Fourth of July, Thanksgiving, Memorial Day, anniversary dates of marriage and of deaths.

At family gatherings, there are empty chairs. The group size is smaller because that special person is absent yearly. Amongst all the joy and laughter, your heart is longing for him/her. You *suffer silently* as others mention their names or show photos of them from previous events.

There are times you may withdraw from interacting or socializing with family and friends. Choosing to stay in bed most of the day, ignoring phone calls, resorting to drinking, or eating a lot, just to get past the hours of the day, seems like the most comforting things to do. You just can't seem to get over the longing because the void is always present.

Just observing the excitement and enjoyment of others, is painful to watch because you are *suffering silently* while missing your loved one or friend.

Have you considered what your absent significant other would want you to do if he/she was still present? These suggestions might help. Try taking a hot shower to relax your mind before attending the event for a short time or perhaps take a friend along for comfort and support.

Reflections (Song/Movie/ Accessories/Articles)

The reflections, of the situation you encountered, stay heavily on your mind. Perhaps it's a song being sung, movie the family is watching, book a friend is reading, or a car the neighbor is driving that caught your attention.

It is possible that being around other people makes the memories too painful to discuss. Once tears became uncontainable, it was definitely time to rush over and change the station or turn the volume down low. Internal crying about the breakup whether it's from separation, divorce, or by death left you feeling hurt, lonely, sadden, frustrate and worried.

Those emotions brought on anxiety by reflecting back to old times. You *suffer silently* wishing your loved ones were still here to enjoy the sound or see the items you are beholding.

Reliving the past can lead to depression or cause long term *silent suffering* for months or years if the surviving ones don't eventually move forward mentally. Although it can be challenging, hopefully the pains will lessen day after day. Always treasure the historical moments in your heart and mind. For mental enjoyment, be thankful for the pleasant times as you hold on to them for strength and comfort.

Revenge

Are you still very hurt from some experiences that caused a deep wound in your heart? Has thoughts of forgery, fighting, or stealing etc. ever entered your mind? Will most personal retaliation lead to some jail time? Are there legal advice agencies available but they charge a high fee?

Feeling like there is no end to this drama has you lying awoke many nights. Weariness from the incident created a great deal of fidgeting and fatigue the next day. Being so mentally outraged about the situation has you *suffering silently* wanting to take matters into your own hands to get a quick revenge. Knowing your mistreatment was unwarranted provided hope that eventually the issue would become a thing of the past.

Here is some advice I would like to personally recommend. Seek free legal aid advice. Keep your distance from people who started the problems. Give those issues over to the Lord in daily prayer. Seek new perspectives, focus on your health/safety and keep moving forward. Stay focused while allowing time and space for justice to occur. Take many deep breaths and always use self control. Surround yourself with positive people who care about your overall well-being.

Mentor/Therapy
Counseling Sessions

Mentors: Someone you trust to tell your secret life of pains, tears, and heartaches. They must be able to listen, without interruptions, being judgmental, or blaming you. They should be patience, sympathetic, loving, supportive, and optimistic. All information shared must be kept strictly confidential. Find someone who could be available should you need to reach out at any time, day or night.

Individual Therapy. This is one on one time with your selected therapist and/or psychologist. Everything is privately discussed. Tell them how you are really feeling, no cover up but open up completely and honestly. They can help relieve anxiety and stress by talking it out privately.

Group Therapy. There are so many others in this world who are currently going or have gone through the very same things you have experienced. The news was devastating, shocking, unbelievable, and almost unbearable. Being in group therapy will show how others are coping and offer tips on ways to better deal with problems and stressful situations.

Seek out professional help. Don't be afraid to open up and speak out on issues that are hurtful and causing you to miserably *suffer silently.*

Suffering Silently
(Life Experiences)

As a result of growing up shy, it later resulted in me becoming a very private person. So, I do not like to share my personal life except to a few chosen people whom I could trust to keep pertinent information confidential. I convey only to those who will listen and join me in prayer over the issues. "Here are some questions I would like to ask to see if anyone has ever encountered any of these things.

We all know life can be challenging and creates difficulties when someone is trying to focus. Finding ways to destress, we seek solitary places indoor and outdoor, looking for an escape from the daily cares of life.

You may have gone to your closet, knelt down or laid on the floor (if there was enough room) or quietly sat in a locked bathroom (until there was an interruption) praying for peace. There are a few other places to choose, as our favorite private spot, when there is a need for some quiet time to meditate, reevaluate, or eliminate.

How often was your crying done under the bedcovers, in the garage, backyard, laundry room, woods etc? Were there times when social media was excessively used as an escape to your mental madness? Did you take your anger or frustration out on others?

Ever cried out to God in desperation for deliverance and peace from the situation? Do these questions sound familiar? Is my faith being tested? How much more pressure can I handle? Can this terrible ordeal work out something good in my favor? Should I wait patiently and prayerfully? Does God see my injustice?"

Has the spirit of loneliness, friendlessness, or carelessness caused you to keep quiet? Regretfully, choosing to remain silent by pretending everything was alright only caused more irritation, agitation, frustration and made you *suffered silently*.

Upon discovering "an unexpected" medical diagnoses in May 2007, I still went to work daily with a smile on my face. Refusing to inform my coworkers the doctors were planning to perform a seven hour operation, for the removal of a benign tumor, left me *suffering silently*. Fearing they may reveal some negative reports about others who had the same procedure done, made me skeptical, so I kept my upcoming surgical appointment a secret for months.

In my family relations, I had to encounter and endure several obstacles. Many lessons were learned about trust, endurance, patience, perseverance, perspective and priority. Through hard times I discovered ways to cope by trusting God and his timing. My encouraging motivators taught me how to control my emotions, focus on my health and safety, ignore certain negative behaviors and people, seek counseling, move forward, and/or find things of interest (hobbies) to engage in. Staying positive and calm are the keys to overcoming obstacles, challenges, interruptions and interferences.

Please do not be afraid to seek medical, legal, financial, educational, psychological, or professional help when necessary. Sometimes we *suffer silently* as a result of our own strong will. Refusing to take the advice of a trusted friend or share our story with others, for various reasons, can cause long term mental and physical illnesses later.

Rest assure that as difficult as it may seem, opening up and disclosing your secret life (revealing the real you behind the mask, makeup, suit, etc) to someone trustworthy, will be the first steps towards healing and recovery.

Holding onto negative hurtful things is very tormenting and can become self destructive.

Release it and be free in every area of your life.

Praying someday soon, after reading my book, you will be inspired to speak out on issues that are causing chaos. Don't *suffer silently* when help is available.

Coping Skills and Strategies

Get involved:

Professional counseling
Prayer groups
Shopping
Reading
Praying
Journaling
Meditation
Art/Crafts
Listen to music
Dinner/Movie
Hobby
Swimming
Exercise
Volunteer
Draw/Paint
Dance
Cook
Sing
Clean/sort items at home
Organize
Visit elderly/sick/friends/family
Plant a garden
Rake the yard
Mow the lawn

Play sport games
Play card games
Wash the car
Write letters
Get your hair/nails/facial done
Go on a mini vacation
Read to children
Research a topic
Call/email/text someone
Inventory
Sort coins

Positive Buzz Words

Commit some of them to memory and repeat ALOUD often as possible:

Faith
Mastery
Resilient
Sufficient
Talk
Destination
Confess
Abundance
Educate
Appreciate
Read
Dream
Self
Blessed
Forgive
Enjoy
Healing
Inspire
Empathy
Beauty
Optimistic
Tropical
Determination
Soothing

Health	Release
Paradise	Rest
Coping	Forward
Ocean	Smile
Fresh	Shift
Start	Envision
Masterpiece	Laughter
Heaven	Mentor
Peace	Freedom
Rewind	Trailblazer
Courageous	Friendship
Reboot	Survival
Wisdom	Happiness
Refocus	
Goals	
Reward	
Recovery	
Rejoice	
Restoration	
Renew	
Believe	
Restore	
Love	
Rebuild	
Relentless	
Relax	
Motivation	
Reevaluate	
Fearless	
Rediscover	
Focus	
Repair	
Positive	
Revisit	
Socialize	
Rise	

About the Author

Sudie (Sue-D) has been married over thirty years to retired Army Sergeant Glenn Williams.

They have one daughter (Peachy) and a son-in-law (Thomas). She also has a grandson (Kamarie) and granddaughter (Jaida).

After earning her bachelor of science in preschool education, she worked as a teacher, assistant director and director of various childcare centers and Head Start programs.

Sudie encounters people, on daily basis, who have a story to tell about their pains and suffering. They are seeking someone who will listen and share advice that brings relief, comfort, hope, and healing.

Sudie is an active listener, and she enjoys making people smile and laugh. Her belief is you should invoke prayer over your problems. She encourages people to think positive thoughts and speak optimistic words over their situations.

In her spare time, Sudie finds pleasure in spending quality time dining out with her family. She enjoys reading, exercising, shopping, socializing with her friends and visiting the sick and elderly. Sudie often spends devoted time listening and praying for others who are hurting and suffering silently.

CPSIA information can be obtained
at www.ICGtesting.com
Printed in the USA
BVHW031748160920
588950BV00001B/38